DAYDREAM DARYL
and the Dental Dilemma

Daryl was at school, and he noticed his friend Kendall was not in class. During recess all the kids were talking about the go-kart race that Daryl won a few days ago. A couple of them said that Kendall had been eating her candy-powered car after the race. Perhaps she was sick after eating too much candy, thought Daryl.

On Daryl's way home he decided to stop by Kendall's house to check on her. When he arrived at her house, he heard a loud scream coming from Kendall's garage. Daryl ran to see what was going on and he found Kendall holding her jaw saying, "mommy my teeth hurt!"

Daryl asked if she was okay, and Kendall's mother said that she had been sneakily eating her candy go-kart for three days and her teeth were hurting. Kendall's mom told Daryl, "Maybe this is not a good time to visit Kendall because she is in a great deal of pain."

Daryl continued to walk home and during his walk he was really worried about his friend. When got home he told his parents that Kendall was having problems with her teeth from eating too much candy.

"Oh, I am sorry to hear about your friend's teeth," said his dad.

Then his mom said, "That reminds me. Daryl, you have a dental appointment tomorrow with the town dentist, Dr. Zidel.

Daryl had also forgotten that he had an appointment with Dr. Zidel. He immediately went to the bathroom to brush his teeth, and Popcorn, his dog, followed him. Talking about the dentist made him think about Kendall even more.

Daryl and Popcorn went to the backyard to play, and, as usual, Daryl started to daydream. This time he dreamed about going to dental school and becoming a world class dentist. In his dream he was able to help children all over the world to prevent cavities, by advising them to not eat so much candy and other sugary food.

Unfortunately, Daydream Daryl's dental practice started to anger the candy makers of the world because children stopped eating so much candy, due to Daryl's popularity and his expert advice. Representatives from all the candy companies stormed into Daryl's office and told all the waiting parents that Daryl could not possibly be a dentist because he was just a kid.

This is when Daryl woke up from his daydream, with Popcorn licking his hand. After his dream he realised how important it was to go to see the dentist regularly, to limit the amount of candy you ate, and brush your teeth regularly. After he had been to see Dr. Zidel, he would call Kendall and tell her she should visit the dentist too.

The next day at Dr. Zidel's office, Daryl was receiving his check up when he heard the same scream from the day before, "Mmommy my teeth hurt!" He knew immediately that it was his friend Kendall, so he told Dr. Zidel about the go-cart race. He mentioned that his friend had made a candy go-kart and that she had eaten half of it in the three days since the race. He told the dentist that Kendall needed help badly.

After he had finished with Daryl's check up, Dr. Zidel took Kendall in for an x-ray of her teeth and found out she had a very bad cavity.

Daryl and Popcorn waited in the lobby until the dentist had finished, to make sure Kendall would be okay. Dr. Zidel removed the tooth with the cavity, and instructed Kendall to ensure she brushed her teeth after every meal, floss, and most importantly, to stop eating so much candy.

Kendall agreed with the dentist that she had been silly to eat the candy go-kart and was so happy that her mouth felt better. Daryl and Popcorn were very relieved that their friend was no longer in pain. Soon, they left the surgery and walked home together.

Kendall asked Daryl to help her build a new go-kart that was not made of candy. He was happy to help her, especially as his own solar-powered go-cart had been so successful.

Then Daryl and Kendall talked about how they would love to be dentists when they grew up and help protect people's teeth from cavities. Until then, they agreed to follow Dr. Zidel's instructions of brushing, flossing, and not eating too much candy.